D0822557

If found, please contact:

_____

_____

THE
3-MINUTE
MORNING
–AND EVENING–

Intentions & Reflections
for a Powerful Life

Publisher's Note

This publication is designed to provide insightful information in regard to the subject matter covered. It is sold with the understanding that neither the publisher nor the author is engaged in rendering coaching, counseling, or other professional services. If expert assistance is needed, the services of a competent professional should be sought.

***

Autumn Creek Press

inquiries@autumncreekpress.com

ISBN-13: 978-1720729914

First Edition

HELLO.

Congratulations on taking the first step toward a more productive, fulfilling, and enjoyable life. Sure, you just purchased a paperback journal, but the simple daily practice you're about to begin will have a profound effect on your life.

The 3-Minute Morning (and evening) is designed to help you begin each morning with intention and gratitude, and retire each evening with reflection and satisfaction. Each and every day on this earth is a gift. It's a blank slate. A fresh start. Yours, to do with it what you will. You are the master of your own life, whether you realize it yet or not. You get to decide how you spend your time, how you see the world, and how you react to different situations, each and every day.

In today's world of constant distraction, there is power in deliberate focus. In today's world of insatiable appetites, there is power in sincere gratitude. And in today's world of self-gratification, there is power in kindness and generosity.

This journal, and the daily practice it promotes, is designed to bring you that power. To help set intentions for each day, keep your mind in a state of gratitude, and identify opportunities for daily kindness. Make this a habit in your daily life, and you'll be surprised at the difference it will make.

HOW TO USE
THIS JOURNAL

Each journal page contains an inspirational quote and four prompts. The first three prompts aid in setting your attitude and intentions for the day and should be pondered and addressed first thing in the morning—ideally before doing anything else. The fourth prompt is designed to help you reflect on and identify personal wins, accomplishments, and events from the day, and should be pondered and addressed at the close of each day, right before bed.

There is no right or wrong way to answer the four prompts—you may use whatever format, and answer in whatever depth, you find most useful. In truth, the only "wrong" way to use this journal is to not use it at all!

You will begin to see the effects of the practice almost immediately. To reap the full benefit from the journal, however, **I encourage you to take a few moments, from time to time, to flip back through the pages and reflect on what you have written.** This might be once a week, every few months, at the close of the year, or during a time of particular difficulty or discouragement. Reflecting on your own handwritten list of accomplishment and positivity is surprisingly motivating. Maintain this as a regular practice, and these little journals will become a source of great encouragement and satisfaction throughout your life.

The Four Prompts

If you're ready to dive in, feel free to skip this section and get right to journaling. If you're looking for a little more guidance, we'll discuss each of the four prompts—and the reasoning behind them—in the section below.

1) "My Life Is Great Because..."

There is a wealth of research demonstrating the positive effects of gratitude. Studies show that taking time each day to specifically identify positive gifts, blessings, circumstances, etc. can significantly improve our overall happiness in life. Cultivating an "attitude of gratitude" can improve our physical health, deepen our sense of connection with others, make us more optimistic, and even increase the length and quality of our sleep.

This prompt is worded differently from other gratitude journals, however, to take advantage of the power of positive thinking. It is all too easy to get caught in the trap of saying "I'll be happy *when...*" and focusing on what we don't have rather than what we do. Your life is already great. You already have a million reasons to be grateful. Reflecting on and responding to this prompt reinforces that truth on a daily basis, replacing thoughts of "I'll be happy *when...*" with the more empowering "I am happy *now.*"

As you prepare to tackle the day, take a moment to express gratitude for what you already have:

My Life Is Great Because:

1. I am healthy.

2. I'm getting together with friends tonight

3. I got a full 8 hours of sleep last night!

You live an incredible life. Enjoy the practice of showing yourself that that's true.

2) "I Will Move Closer to My Goals Today By..."

Most people try to do *far* more in a day than is possible. To-do lists run over with a seemingly endless stream of tasks, and even our best efforts fall short of truly getting "everything" done that we want to.

If you really scrutinized the items on your list, though, how many of them *really* need to get done? What one, two, or three items on there are going to bring you the most bang for your buck? And—most importantly—**which one, two, or three items will actually take you closer to your major life goals?**

I recommend keeping your work to-do list out of this morning reflection, unless your current job relates to or helps achieve your long-term goals. For most of us, our "must-do" list is driven by our day jobs, and by the time we sit down to focus on personal and/or longer-term objectives (e.g. starting a side hustle, spending more time with the kids, drafting a manuscript for a new book, etc.), we're out of energy or have otherwise lost sight of what we really want.

This prompt is intended to refocus you on your longer-term goals and help identify specific actions you can take each day to achieve them.

If you don't already have clear goals for the year (and beyond), I strongly recommend you take time this week to set them. Print them out and post them somewhere in your room so you see them every day. Then, when you sit down with this journal each morning, take a glance at those goals and think of a few specific actions you can take that day to move closer to achieving them:

I Will Move Closer to My Goals Today By:

1.   Finding 10 potential leads for my side business

2.   Drafting one blog post

3.   Exercising for at least 30 minutes

You can always accomplish more, but setting clear intentions at the beginning of each day will 1) train your brain to identify high-value and low-value tasks, 2) keep you focused on the most important items throughout the day, and 3) set you up for feelings of accomplishment, rather than overwhelm, at the end of each day.

3) "Today I Will Brighten _____'s Day..."

The third prompt—my favorite—encourages you to look outward, think of people you interact with day-to-day, and make a plan to intentionally help, compliment, strengthen, or support at least one individual.

This is a powerful practice, as it's been proven time and

time again that acts of service generate a significant happiness boost in the giver. (And it goes without saying that they brighten the day of the recipient as well!)

For this prompt, think of a specific person, a specific way to brighten their day, and commit to take action:

Today I Will Brighten _____*Steven*_____ **'s Day By:**

 telling him how much I appreciate our friendship.

If you find yourself at a loss for a specific name, feel free to use a category or broader description, such as "a sibling," "a coworker," or even "a stranger." If you take this approach, though, still think of a specific way you can help. For example, if you're heading to dinner that evening, you might write:

Today I Will Brighten _____*our server*_____ **'s Day By:**

 tipping a few dollars extra.

A little kindness goes a long way. I can tell you from personal experience that setting this intention each morning, and acting on it, will make a *significant* impact on your life.

4) "Today Was Great Because..."

The fourth and final prompt encourages you to reflect on the day and identify a few wins, accomplishments, or other positive events from the day. This practice closes out the day with simple-yet-satisfying mix of gratitude, fulfillment, and confidence.

"But what if today *wasn't* great?" you ask. This prompt is

9

worded the way it is for a reason, and it's *especially* valuable on days you consider pretty rotten. The truth is, we all live amazing lives. If you have clean water to drink, a roof over your head, and family or friends to talk to, you have significantly more than most in this world. Even if you suffered a terrible tragedy, I guarantee there were positive events surrounding it. Perhaps you had friends reach out to help, perhaps the bad situation could have been even worse, and so forth. Give this prompt a few minutes of thought and you will *always* find reasons to be grateful.

Today Was Great Because:

1. I got that presentation finished

2. I helped my sister deal with her frustration with Brian

3. I made it to the gym!

Reflecting back on this prompt can also be insightful after you've collected several months of entries. Are there patterns or themes in what you've written? Can you identify actions or events that consistently bring you joy? If so, what can you do to invite more of those into your life?

Let's get into it.

THE 3-MINUTE MORNING

MORNING

–AND EVENING–

Date: ___ / ___ / _____

"I attribute my success to this: I never
gave or took any excuse."

— *Florence Nightingale*

My Life Is Great Because:

1. _____

2. _____

3. _____

I Will Move Closer to My Goals Today By:

1. _____

2. _____

3. _____

Today I Will Brighten _____**'s Day By:**

_____

_____

* * *

Today Was Great Because:

1. _____

2. _____

3. _____

Date: ___ / ___ / _____

"I am not a product of my circumstances.
I am a product of my decisions."

– *Stephen Covey*

My Life Is Great Because:

1. _____
2. _____
3. _____

I Will Move Closer to My Goals Today By:

1. _____
2. _____
3. _____

Today I Will Brighten _____'s Day By:

_____

_____

* * *

Today Was Great Because:

1. _____
2. _____
3. _____

Date: ___ / ___ / _____

"I've learned that people will forget what you said, people
will forget what you did, but people will
never forget how you made them feel."

– Maya Angelou

My Life Is Great Because:

1. _____
2. _____
3. _____

I Will Move Closer to My Goals Today By:

1. _____
2. _____
3. _____

Today I Will Brighten _____'s Day By:

_____

_____

* * *

Today Was Great Because:

1. _____
2. _____
3. _____

Date: ___ / ___ / _____

"You can do anything,
but you can't do everything."
— *David Allen*

My Life Is Great Because:

1. _____

2. _____

3. _____

I Will Move Closer to My Goals Today By:

1. _____

2. _____

3. _____

Today I Will Brighten _____'s Day By:

_____

_____

* * *

Today Was Great Because:

1. _____

2. _____

3. _____

Date: ___ / ___ / _____

"Life shrinks or expands in
proportion to one's courage."

– Anais Nin

My Life Is Great Because:

1. _____
2. _____
3. _____

I Will Move Closer to My Goals Today By:

1. _____
2. _____
3. _____

Today I Will Brighten _____**'s Day By:**

_____

_____

* * *

Today Was Great Because:

1. _____
2. _____
3. _____

Date: ___ / ___ / _____

"Great spirits have always found violent
opposition from mediocre minds."
— *Albert Einstein*

My Life Is Great Because:

1. _____
2. _____
3. _____

I Will Move Closer to My Goals Today By:

1. _____
2. _____
3. _____

Today I Will Brighten _____'s Day By:

_____

_____

* * *

Today Was Great Because:

1. _____
2. _____
3. _____

Date: ___ / ___ / _____

> "Overcome the notion that you must be regular. It robs
> you of the chance to be extraordinary."
>
> – *Uta Hagen*

My Life Is Great Because:

1. _____
2. _____
3. _____

I Will Move Closer to My Goals Today By:

1. _____
2. _____
3. _____

Today I Will Brighten _____'s Day By:

_____

_____

* * *

Today Was Great Because:

1. _____
2. _____
3. _____

Date: ___ / ___ / _____

"Whatever the mind of man can conceive
and believe, it can achieve."
– *Napoleon Hill*

My Life Is Great Because:

1. _____
2. _____
3. _____

I Will Move Closer to My Goals Today By:

1. _____
2. _____
3. _____

Today I Will Brighten _____'s Day By:

_____

_____

* * *

Today Was Great Because:

1. _____
2. _____
3. _____

Date: ___ / ___ / _____

"Strive not to be a success, but
rather to be of value."

— *Albert Einstein*

My Life Is Great Because:

1. _____

2. _____

3. _____

I Will Move Closer to My Goals Today By:

1. _____

2. _____

3. _____

Today I Will Brighten _____**'s Day By:**

_____

_____

* * *

Today Was Great Because:

1. _____

2. _____

3. _____

Date: ___ / ___ / _____

"Two roads diverged in a wood, and I—I took the one less traveled by, and that has made all the difference."
— *Robert Frost*

My Life Is Great Because:

1. _____

2. _____

3. _____

I Will Move Closer to My Goals Today By:

1. _____

2. _____

3. _____

Today I Will Brighten _____'s Day By:

_____

_____

***

Today Was Great Because:

1. _____

2. _____

3. _____

Date: ___ / ___ / _____

"You miss 100% of the shots you don't take."
— *Wayne Gretzky*

My Life Is Great Because:

1. _____

2. _____

3. _____

I Will Move Closer to My Goals Today By:

1. _____

2. _____

3. _____

Today I Will Brighten _____**'s Day By:**

_____

_____

* * *

Today Was Great Because:

1. _____

2. _____

3. _____

Date: ___ / ___ / _____

"The most difficult thing is the decision to act,
the rest is merely tenacity."

– *Amelia Earhart*

My Life Is Great Because:

1. _____

2. _____

3. _____

I Will Move Closer to My Goals Today By:

1. _____

2. _____

3. _____

Today I Will Brighten _____'s Day By:

_____

_____

* * *

Today Was Great Because:

1. _____

2. _____

3. _____

Date: ___ / ___ / _____

"Every strike brings me closer to the next home run."
— *Babe Ruth*

My Life Is Great Because:

1. _____

2. _____

3. _____

I Will Move Closer to My Goals Today By:

1. _____

2. _____

3. _____

Today I Will Brighten _____**'s Day By:**

_____

_____

* * *

Today Was Great Because:

1. _____

2. _____

3. _____

Date: ___ / ___ / _____

"Definiteness of purpose is the starting
point of all achievement."

– W. Clement Stone

My Life Is Great Because:

1. _____

2. _____

3. _____

I Will Move Closer to My Goals Today By:

1. _____

2. _____

3. _____

Today I Will Brighten _____'s Day By:

_____

_____

* * *

Today Was Great Because:

1. _____

2. _____

3. _____

Date: ___ / ___ / _____

"Life isn't about getting and having,
it's about giving and being."
— Kevin Kruse

My Life Is Great Because:

1. _____

2. _____

3. _____

I Will Move Closer to My Goals Today By:

1. _____

2. _____

3. _____

Today I Will Brighten _____**'s Day By:**

_____

_____

* * *

Today Was Great Because:

1. _____

2. _____

3. _____

Date: ___ / ___ / _____

"Life is what happens to you while
you're busy making other plans."

— John Lennon

My Life Is Great Because:

1. _____
2. _____
3. _____

I Will Move Closer to My Goals Today By:

1. _____
2. _____
3. _____

Today I Will Brighten _____'s Day By:

_____

_____

$$* * *$$

Today Was Great Because:

1. _____
2. _____
3. _____

Date: ___ / ___ / _____

"We become what we think about."

– Earl Nightingale

My Life Is Great Because:

1. _____

2. _____

3. _____

I Will Move Closer to My Goals Today By:

1. _____

2. _____

3. _____

Today I Will Brighten _____'s Day By:

_____

_____

* * *

Today Was Great Because:

1. _____

2. _____

3. _____

Date: ___ / ___ / _____

"Twenty years from now you will be more disappointed by
the things that you didn't do than by the ones you did do."

– Mark Twain

My Life Is Great Because:

1. _____
2. _____
3. _____

I Will Move Closer to My Goals Today By:

1. _____
2. _____
3. _____

Today I Will Brighten _____'s Day By:

_____

_____

* * *

Today Was Great Because:

1. _____
2. _____
3. _____

Date: ___ / ___ / _____

"Life is 10% what happens to me and
90% of how I react to it."
— *Charles Swindoll*

My Life Is Great Because:

1. _____

2. _____

3. _____

I Will Move Closer to My Goals Today By:

1. _____

2. _____

3. _____

Today I Will Brighten _____'s Day By:

_____

_____

* * *

Today Was Great Because:

1. _____

2. _____

3. _____

Date: ___ / ___ / _____

"The most common way people give up their power
is by thinking they don't have any."
— Alice Walker

My Life Is Great Because:

1. _____

2. _____

3. _____

I Will Move Closer to My Goals Today By:

1. _____

2. _____

3. _____

Today I Will Brighten _____**'s Day By:**

_____

_____

* * *

Today Was Great Because:

1. _____

2. _____

3. _____

Date: ___ / ___ / _____

"The mind is everything. What you think you become."
— *Buddha*

My Life Is Great Because:

1. _____
2. _____
3. _____

I Will Move Closer to My Goals Today By:

1. _____
2. _____
3. _____

Today I Will Brighten _____'s Day By:

_____

_____

* * *

Today Was Great Because:

1. _____
2. _____
3. _____

Date: ___ / ___ / _____

"The best time to plant a tree was 20 years ago.
The second-best time is now."

– Chinese Proverb

My Life Is Great Because:

1. _____

2. _____

3. _____

I Will Move Closer to My Goals Today By:

1. _____

2. _____

3. _____

Today I Will Brighten _____'s Day By:

_____

_____

* * *

Today Was Great Because:

1. _____

2. _____

3. _____

34

Date: ___ / ___ / _____

"An unexamined life is not worth living."

— Socrates

My Life Is Great Because:

1. _____
2. _____
3. _____

I Will Move Closer to My Goals Today By:

1. _____
2. _____
3. _____

Today I Will Brighten _____'s Day By:

_____

_____

* * *

Today Was Great Because:

1. _____
2. _____
3. _____

Date: ___ / ___ / _____

"Eighty percent of success is showing up."
— *Woody Allen*

My Life Is Great Because:

1. _____
2. _____
3. _____

I Will Move Closer to My Goals Today By:

1. _____
2. _____
3. _____

Today I Will Brighten _____'s Day By:

_____

_____

* * *

Today Was Great Because:

1. _____
2. _____
3. _____

Date: ___ / ___ / _____

"Your time is limited, so don't waste it
living someone else's life."

— *Steve Jobs*

My Life Is Great Because:

1. _____

2. _____

3. _____

I Will Move Closer to My Goals Today By:

1. _____

2. _____

3. _____

Today I Will Brighten _____**'s Day By:**

_____

_____

* * *

Today Was Great Because:

1. _____

2. _____

3. _____

Date: ___ / ___ / _____

"Every child is an artist. The problem is how
to remain an artist once he grows up."
— *Pablo Picasso*

My Life Is Great Because:

1. _____
2. _____
3. _____

I Will Move Closer to My Goals Today By:

1. _____
2. _____
3. _____

Today I Will Brighten _____'s Day By:

_____

_____

* * *

Today Was Great Because:

1. _____
2. _____
3. _____

Date: ___ / ___ / _____

"You can never cross the ocean until you have
the courage to lose sight of the shore."

— Christopher Columbus

My Life Is Great Because:

1. _____

2. _____

3. _____

I Will Move Closer to My Goals Today By:

1. _____

2. _____

3. _____

Today I Will Brighten _____'s Day By:

_____

_____

* * *

Today Was Great Because:

1. _____

2. _____

3. _____

Date: ___ / ___ / _____

"I attribute my success to this: I never
gave or took any excuse."
— *Florence Nightingale*

My Life Is Great Because:

1. _____

2. _____

3. _____

I Will Move Closer to My Goals Today By:

1. _____

2. _____

3. _____

Today I Will Brighten _____'s Day By:

_____

_____

* * *

Today Was Great Because:

1. _____

2. _____

3. _____

Date: ___ / ___ / _____

"Either you run the day, or the day runs you."
— *Jim Rohn*

My Life Is Great Because:

1. _____

2. _____

3. _____

I Will Move Closer to My Goals Today By:

1. _____

2. _____

3. _____

Today I Will Brighten _____'s Day By:

_____

_____

* * *

Today Was Great Because:

1. _____

2. _____

3. _____

Date: ___ / ___ / _____

"Whether you think you can or you
think you can't, you're right."

– Henry Ford

My Life Is Great Because:

1. _____
2. _____
3. _____

I Will Move Closer to My Goals Today By:

1. _____
2. _____
3. _____

Today I Will Brighten _____**'s Day By:**

_____

_____

* * *

Today Was Great Because:

1. _____
2. _____
3. _____

Date: ___ / ___ / _____

"The two most important days in your life are the day
you are born and the day you find out why."

– Mark Twain

My Life Is Great Because:

1. _____
2. _____
3. _____

I Will Move Closer to My Goals Today By:

1. _____
2. _____
3. _____

Today I Will Brighten _____'s Day By:

_____

_____

* * *

Today Was Great Because:

1. _____
2. _____
3. _____

Date: ___ / ___ / _____

"Whatever you can do, or dream you can, begin it.
Boldness has genius, power and magic in it."
— *Johann Wolfgang von Goethe*

My Life Is Great Because:

1. _____
2. _____
3. _____

I Will Move Closer to My Goals Today By:

1. _____
2. _____
3. _____

Today I Will Brighten _____'s Day By:

_____

_____

* * *

Today Was Great Because:

1. _____
2. _____
3. _____

Date: ___ / ___ / _____

"People often say that motivation doesn't last. Well, neither does bathing. That's why we recommend it daily."

– Zig Ziglar

My Life Is Great Because:

1. _____
2. _____
3. _____

I Will Move Closer to My Goals Today By:

1. _____
2. _____
3. _____

Today I Will Brighten _____**'s Day By:**

_____

_____

* * *

Today Was Great Because:

1. _____
2. _____
3. _____

Date: ___ / ___ / _____

"If you hear a voice within you say 'you cannot paint,' then by all means paint and that voice will be silenced."

– Vincent Van Gogh

My Life Is Great Because:

1. _____
2. _____
3. _____

I Will Move Closer to My Goals Today By:

1. _____
2. _____
3. _____

Today I Will Brighten _____'s Day By:

_____

_____

***

Today Was Great Because:

1. _____
2. _____
3. _____

Date: ___ / ___ / _____

"There is only one way to avoid criticism: do nothing,
say nothing, and be nothing."

– Aristotle

My Life Is Great Because:

1. _____

2. _____

3. _____

I Will Move Closer to My Goals Today By:

1. _____

2. _____

3. _____

Today I Will Brighten _____**'s Day By:**

_____

_____

* * *

Today Was Great Because:

1. _____

2. _____

3. _____

Date: ___ / ___ / _____

"Ask and it will be given to you; search, and you will find;
knock and the door will be opened for you."

— Jesus

My Life Is Great Because:

1. _____
2. _____
3. _____

I Will Move Closer to My Goals Today By:

1. _____
2. _____
3. _____

Today I Will Brighten _____'s Day By:

_____

_____

* * *

Today Was Great Because:

1. _____
2. _____
3. _____

Date: ___ / ___ / _____

"The only person you are destined to
become is the person you decide to be.
– *Ralph Waldo Emerson*

My Life Is Great Because:

1. _____

2. _____

3. _____

I Will Move Closer to My Goals Today By:

1. _____

2. _____

3. _____

Today I Will Brighten _____'s Day By:

_____

_____

* * *

Today Was Great Because:

1. _____

2. _____

3. _____

Date: ___ / ___ / _____

"Go confidently in the direction of your dreams.
Live the life you have imagined."

– Henry David Thoreau

My Life Is Great Because:

1. _____
2. _____
3. _____

I Will Move Closer to My Goals Today By:

1. _____
2. _____
3. _____

Today I Will Brighten _____'s Day By:

_____

_____

* * *

Today Was Great Because:

1. _____
2. _____
3. _____

Date: ___ / ___ / _____

"When I stand before God at the end of my life, I would
hope that I would not have a single bit of talent left and
could say, I used everything you gave me."

– Erma Bombeck

My Life Is Great Because:

1. _____

2. _____

3. _____

I Will Move Closer to My Goals Today By:

1. _____

2. _____

3. _____

Today I Will Brighten _____'s Day By:

_____

_____

* * *

Today Was Great Because:

1. _____

2. _____

3. _____

Date: ___ / ___ / _____

"Few things can help an individual more than to place
responsibility on him, and to let him know
that you trust him."

— Booker T. Washington

My Life Is Great Because:

1. _____

2. _____

3. _____

I Will Move Closer to My Goals Today By:

1. _____

2. _____

3. _____

Today I Will Brighten _____'s Day By:

_____

_____

* * *

Today Was Great Because:

1. _____

2. _____

3. _____

Date: ___ / ___ / _____

"Certain things catch your eye, but pursue
only those that capture the heart."

— Ancient Indian Proverb

My Life Is Great Because:

1. _____

2. _____

3. _____

I Will Move Closer to My Goals Today By:

1. _____

2. _____

3. _____

Today I Will Brighten _____**'s Day By:**

_____

_____

* * *

Today Was Great Because:

1. _____

2. _____

3. _____

Date: ___ / ___ / _____

"Believe you can and you're halfway there."
— *Theodore Roosevelt*

My Life Is Great Because:

1. _____

2. _____

3. _____

I Will Move Closer to My Goals Today By:

1. _____

2. _____

3. _____

Today I Will Brighten _____**'s Day By:**

_____

_____

* * *

Today Was Great Because:

1. _____

2. _____

3. _____

Date: ___ / ___ / _____

"Everything you've ever wanted is on
the other side of fear."

– *George Addair*

My Life Is Great Because:

1. _____

2. _____

3. _____

I Will Move Closer to My Goals Today By:

1. _____

2. _____

3. _____

Today I Will Brighten _____'s Day By:

_____

_____

* * *

Today Was Great Because:

1. _____

2. _____

3. _____

Date: ___ / ___ / _____

"We can easily forgive a child who is afraid of the dark; the real tragedy of life is when men are afraid of the light."

— Plato

My Life Is Great Because:

1. _____
2. _____
3. _____

I Will Move Closer to My Goals Today By:

1. _____
2. _____
3. _____

Today I Will Brighten _____**'s Day By:**

_____

_____

* * *

Today Was Great Because:

1. _____
2. _____
3. _____

Date: ___ / ___ / _____

"Teach thy tongue to say, 'I do not know,'
and thou shalt progress."

– Maimonides

My Life Is Great Because:

1. _____

2. _____

3. _____

I Will Move Closer to My Goals Today By:

1. _____

2. _____

3. _____

Today I Will Brighten _____**'s Day By:**

_____

_____

* * *

Today Was Great Because:

1. _____

2. _____

3. _____

Date: ___ / ___ / _____

"Start where you are.
Use what you have.
Do what you can."

– Arthur Ashe

My Life Is Great Because:

1. _____

2. _____

3. _____

I Will Move Closer to My Goals Today By:

1. _____

2. _____

3. _____

Today I Will Brighten _____'s Day By:

_____

_____

* * *

Today Was Great Because:

1. _____

2. _____

3. _____

Date: ___ / ___ / _____

"Fall seven times and stand up eight."
— *Japanese Proverb*

My Life Is Great Because:

1. _____

2. _____

3. _____

I Will Move Closer to My Goals Today By:

1. _____

2. _____

3. _____

Today I Will Brighten _____**'s Day By:**

_____

_____

* * *

Today Was Great Because:

1. _____

2. _____

3. _____

Date: ___ / ___ / _____

"When one door of happiness closes, another opens, but often we look so long at the closed door that we do not see the one that has been opened for us."

– Helen Keller

My Life Is Great Because:

1. _____

2. _____

3. _____

I Will Move Closer to My Goals Today By:

1. _____

2. _____

3. _____

Today I Will Brighten _____'s Day By:

_____

_____

* * *

Today Was Great Because:

1. _____

2. _____

3. _____

Date: ___ / ___ / _____

"How wonderful it is that nobody need wait a single moment before starting to improve the world."

— *Anne Frank*

My Life Is Great Because:

1. _____

2. _____

3. _____

I Will Move Closer to My Goals Today By:

1. _____

2. _____

3. _____

Today I Will Brighten _____**'s Day By:**

_____

_____

* * *

Today Was Great Because:

1. _____

2. _____

3. _____

Date: ___ / ___ / _____

"When I let go of what I am,
I become what I might be."

– Lao Tzu

My Life Is Great Because:

1. _____

2. _____

3. _____

I Will Move Closer to My Goals Today By:

1. _____

2. _____

3. _____

Today I Will Brighten _____'s Day By:

_____

_____

* * *

Today Was Great Because:

1. _____

2. _____

3. _____

Date: ___ / ___ / _____

"Happiness is not something readymade.
It comes from your own actions."

– *Dalai Lama*

My Life Is Great Because:

1. _____
2. _____
3. _____

I Will Move Closer to My Goals Today By:

1. _____
2. _____
3. _____

Today I Will Brighten _____**'s Day By:**

_____

_____

* * *

Today Was Great Because:

1. _____
2. _____
3. _____

Date: ___ / ___ / _____

"If the wind will not serve, take to the oars."

– Latin Proverb

My Life Is Great Because:

1. _____

2. _____

3. _____

I Will Move Closer to My Goals Today By:

1. _____

2. _____

3. _____

Today I Will Brighten _____**'s Day By:**

_____

_____

* * *

Today Was Great Because:

1. _____

2. _____

3. _____

Date: ___ / ___ / _____

"You can't fall if you don't climb. But there's no joy in
living your whole life on the ground."

– Unknown

My Life Is Great Because:

1. _____

2. _____

3. _____

I Will Move Closer to My Goals Today By:

1. _____

2. _____

3. _____

Today I Will Brighten _____**'s Day By:**

_____

_____

* * *

Today Was Great Because:

1. _____

2. _____

3. _____

Date: ___ / ___ / _____

"We must believe that we are gifted for something, and that
this thing, at whatever cost, must be attained."

– Marie Curie

My Life Is Great Because:

1. _____

2. _____

3. _____

I Will Move Closer to My Goals Today By:

1. _____

2. _____

3. _____

Today I Will Brighten _____'s Day By:

_____

_____

* * *

Today Was Great Because:

1. _____

2. _____

3. _____

Date: ___ / ___ / _____

"Too many of us are not living our dreams
because we are living our fears."

– Les Brown

My Life Is Great Because:

1. _____
2. _____
3. _____

I Will Move Closer to My Goals Today By:

1. _____
2. _____
3. _____

Today I Will Brighten _____'s Day By:

_____

_____

* * *

Today Was Great Because:

1. _____
2. _____
3. _____

Date: ___ / ___ / _____

"Challenges are what make life interesting and overcoming
them is what makes life meaningful."

– Joshua J. Marine

My Life Is Great Because:

1. _____
2. _____
3. _____

I Will Move Closer to My Goals Today By:

1. _____
2. _____
3. _____

Today I Will Brighten _____'s Day By:

_____

_____

***

Today Was Great Because:

1. _____
2. _____
3. _____

Date: ___ / ___ / _____

"If you want to lift yourself up, lift up someone else."
– Booker T. Washington

My Life Is Great Because:

1. _____

2. _____

3. _____

I Will Move Closer to My Goals Today By:

1. _____

2. _____

3. _____

Today I Will Brighten _____'s Day By:

_____

_____

* * *

Today Was Great Because:

1. _____

2. _____

3. _____

Date: ___ / ___ / _____

"I have been impressed with the urgency of doing.
Knowing is not enough; we must apply.
Being willing is not enough; we must do."

— Leonardo da Vinci

My Life Is Great Because:

1. _____
2. _____
3. _____

I Will Move Closer to My Goals Today By:

1. _____
2. _____
3. _____

Today I Will Brighten _____'s Day By:

_____

_____

* * *

Today Was Great Because:

1. _____
2. _____
3. _____

Date: ___ / ___ / _____

"Limitations live only in our minds. But if we use our
imaginations, our possibilities become limitless."
– Jamie Paolinetti

My Life Is Great Because:

1. _____
2. _____
3. _____

I Will Move Closer to My Goals Today By:

1. _____
2. _____
3. _____

Today I Will Brighten _____'s Day By:

_____
_____

***

Today Was Great Because:

1. _____
2. _____
3. _____

71

Date: ___ / ___ / _____

"I've learned that people will forget what you said, people
will forget what you did, but people will
never forget how you made them feel."

– Maya Angelou

My Life Is Great Because:

1. _____

2. _____

3. _____

I Will Move Closer to My Goals Today By:

1. _____

2. _____

3. _____

Today I Will Brighten _____'s Day By:

_____

_____

* * *

Today Was Great Because:

1. _____

2. _____

3. _____

Date: ___ / ___ / _____

"You take your life in your own hands, and what happens?
A terrible thing, no one to blame."

– Erica Jong

My Life Is Great Because:

1. _____

2. _____

3. _____

I Will Move Closer to My Goals Today By:

1. _____

2. _____

3. _____

Today I Will Brighten _____**'s Day By:**

_____

_____

* * *

Today Was Great Because:

1. _____

2. _____

3. _____

Date: ___ / ___ / _____

"What's money? A man is a success if he gets up in the
morning and goes to bed at night and in between
does what he wants to do."

– Bob Dylan

My Life Is Great Because:

1. _____

2. _____

3. _____

I Will Move Closer to My Goals Today By:

1. _____

2. _____

3. _____

Today I Will Brighten _____'s Day By:

_____

_____

* * *

Today Was Great Because:

1. _____

2. _____

3. _____

Date: ___ / ___ / _____

"I didn't fail the test. I just found 100 ways to do it wrong."
— *Benjamin Franklin*

My Life Is Great Because:

1. _____
2. _____
3. _____

I Will Move Closer to My Goals Today By:

1. _____
2. _____
3. _____

Today I Will Brighten _____**'s Day By:**

_____

_____

* * *

Today Was Great Because:

1. _____
2. _____
3. _____

Date: ___ / ___ / _____

"I attribute my success to this: I never
gave or took any excuse."

– *Florence Nightingale*

My Life Is Great Because:

1. _____

2. _____

3. _____

I Will Move Closer to My Goals Today By:

1. _____

2. _____

3. _____

Today I Will Brighten _____'s Day By:

_____

_____

* * *

Today Was Great Because:

1. _____

2. _____

3. _____

Date: ___ / ___ / _____

"A person who never made a mistake
never tried anything new."
– *Albert Einstein*

My Life Is Great Because:

1. _____
2. _____
3. _____

I Will Move Closer to My Goals Today By:

1. _____
2. _____
3. _____

Today I Will Brighten _____'s Day By:

_____

_____

* * *

Today Was Great Because:

1. _____
2. _____
3. _____

Date: ___ / ___ / _____

"The person who says it cannot be done should not interrupt the person who is doing it."

— *Chinese Proverb*

My Life Is Great Because:

1. _____
2. _____
3. _____

I Will Move Closer to My Goals Today By:

1. _____
2. _____
3. _____

Today I Will Brighten _____**'s Day By:**

_____

_____

* * *

Today Was Great Because:

1. _____
2. _____
3. _____

Date: ___ / ___ / _____

"There are no traffic jams along the extra mile."
— *Roger Staubach*

My Life Is Great Because:

1. _____

2. _____

3. _____

I Will Move Closer to My Goals Today By:

1. _____

2. _____

3. _____

Today I Will Brighten _____'s Day By:

_____

_____

* * *

Today Was Great Because:

1. _____

2. _____

3. _____

Date: ___ / ___ / _____

"It is never too late to be what you might have been."

– George Eliot

My Life Is Great Because:

1. _____

2. _____

3. _____

I Will Move Closer to My Goals Today By:

1. _____

2. _____

3. _____

Today I Will Brighten _____'s Day By:

_____

_____

* * *

Today Was Great Because:

1. _____

2. _____

3. _____

Date: ___ / ___ / _____

"Build your own dreams, or someone else
will hire you to build theirs."

– Farrah Gray

My Life Is Great Because:

1. _____

2. _____

3. _____

I Will Move Closer to My Goals Today By:

1. _____

2. _____

3. _____

Today I Will Brighten _____**'s Day By:**

_____

_____

* * *

Today Was Great Because:

1. _____

2. _____

3. _____

Date: ___ / ___ / _____

"Education costs money.
But then so does ignorance."
— *Sir Claus Moser*

My Life Is Great Because:

1. _____
2. _____
3. _____

I Will Move Closer to My Goals Today By:

1. _____
2. _____
3. _____

Today I Will Brighten _____'s Day By:

_____

_____

***

Today Was Great Because:

1. _____
2. _____
3. _____

Date: ___ / ___ / _____

"I have learned over the years that when one's mind is
made up, this diminishes fear."

— Rosa Parks

My Life Is Great Because:

1. _____
2. _____
3. _____

I Will Move Closer to My Goals Today By:

1. _____
2. _____
3. _____

Today I Will Brighten _____'s Day By:

_____

_____

* * *

Today Was Great Because:

1. _____
2. _____
3. _____

Date: ___ / ___ / _____

"It does not matter how slowly you go as
long as you do not stop."

— Confucius

My Life Is Great Because:

1. _____

2. _____

3. _____

I Will Move Closer to My Goals Today By:

1. _____

2. _____

3. _____

Today I Will Brighten _____'s Day By:

_____

_____

* * *

Today Was Great Because:

1. _____

2. _____

3. _____

Date: ___ / ___ / _____

"If you look at what you have in life, you'll always have more. If you look at what you don't have in life, you'll never have enough."

– Oprah Winfrey

My Life Is Great Because:

1. _____

2. _____

3. _____

I Will Move Closer to My Goals Today By:

1. _____

2. _____

3. _____

Today I Will Brighten _____**'s Day By:**

_____

_____

* * *

Today Was Great Because:

1. _____

2. _____

3. _____

Date: ___ / ___ / _____

"Remember that not getting what you want is
sometimes a wonderful stroke of luck."

– *Dalai Lama*

My Life Is Great Because:

1. _____

2. _____

3. _____

I Will Move Closer to My Goals Today By:

1. _____

2. _____

3. _____

Today I Will Brighten _____**'s Day By:**

_____

_____

* * *

Today Was Great Because:

1. _____

2. _____

3. _____

Date: ___ / ___ / _____

"You can't use up creativity.
The more you use, the more you have."
– *Maya Angelou*

My Life Is Great Because:

1. _____
2. _____
3. _____

I Will Move Closer to My Goals Today By:

1. _____
2. _____
3. _____

Today I Will Brighten _____'s Day By:

_____

_____

* * *

Today Was Great Because:

1. _____
2. _____
3. _____

Date: ___ / ___ / _____

"Dream big and dare to fail."
– *Norman Vaughan*

My Life Is Great Because:

1. _____

2. _____

3. _____

I Will Move Closer to My Goals Today By:

1. _____

2. _____

3. _____

Today I Will Brighten _____'s Day By:

_____

_____

* * *

Today Was Great Because:

1. _____

2. _____

3. _____

Date: ___ / ___ / _____

"Our lives begin to end the day we become
silent about things that matter."
– *Martin Luther King Jr.*

My Life Is Great Because:

1. _____

2. _____

3. _____

I Will Move Closer to My Goals Today By:

1. _____

2. _____

3. _____

Today I Will Brighten _____'s Day By:

_____

_____

* * *

Today Was Great Because:

1. _____

2. _____

3. _____

Date: ___ / ___ / _____

"Do what you can, where you are, with what you have."
— Teddy Roosevelt

My Life Is Great Because:

1. _____

2. _____

3. _____

I Will Move Closer to My Goals Today By:

1. _____

2. _____

3. _____

Today I Will Brighten _____'s Day By:

_____

_____

* * *

Today Was Great Because:

1. _____

2. _____

3. _____

Date: ___ / ___ / _____

"If you always do what you've always done,
you'll always get what you've always gotten."
— *Jessie Potter*

My Life Is Great Because:

1. _____

2. _____

3. _____

I Will Move Closer to My Goals Today By:

1. _____

2. _____

3. _____

Today I Will Brighten _____'s Day By:

_____

_____

* * *

Today Was Great Because:

1. _____

2. _____

3. _____

Date: ___ / ___ / _____

"It's your place in the world; it's your life. Go on and do all
you can with it, and make it the life you want to live."

— Mae Jemison

My Life Is Great Because:

1. _____

2. _____

3. _____

I Will Move Closer to My Goals Today By:

1. _____

2. _____

3. _____

Today I Will Brighten _____**'s Day By:**

_____

_____

* * *

Today Was Great Because:

1. _____

2. _____

3. _____

Date: ___ / ___ / _____

"You may be disappointed if you fail, but
you are doomed if you don't try."
— Beverly Sills

My Life Is Great Because:

1. _____

2. _____

3. _____

I Will Move Closer to My Goals Today By:

1. _____

2. _____

3. _____

Today I Will Brighten _____'s Day By:

_____

_____

* * *

Today Was Great Because:

1. _____

2. _____

3. _____

Date: ___ / ___ / _____

"Remember no one can make you feel
inferior without your consent."

– Eleanor Roosevelt

My Life Is Great Because:

1. _____
2. _____
3. _____

I Will Move Closer to My Goals Today By:

1. _____
2. _____
3. _____

Today I Will Brighten _____'s Day By:

_____

_____

* * *

Today Was Great Because:

1. _____
2. _____
3. _____

Date: ___ / ___ / _____

"Life is what we make it, always has been, always will be."

— *Grandma Moses*

My Life Is Great Because:

1. _____

2. _____

3. _____

I Will Move Closer to My Goals Today By:

1. _____

2. _____

3. _____

Today I Will Brighten _____'s Day By:

_____

_____

* * *

Today Was Great Because:

1. _____

2. _____

3. _____

Date: ___ / ___ / _____

*"The question isn't who is going to let me;
it's who is going to stop me."*

– Ayn Rand

My Life Is Great Because:

1. _____

2. _____

3. _____

I Will Move Closer to My Goals Today By:

1. _____

2. _____

3. _____

Today I Will Brighten _____**'s Day By:**

_____

_____

* * *

Today Was Great Because:

1. _____

2. _____

3. _____

Date: ___ / ___ / _____

"When everything seems to be going against you,
remember that the airplane takes off
against the wind, not with it."

– Henry Ford

My Life Is Great Because:

1. _____

2. _____

3. _____

I Will Move Closer to My Goals Today By:

1. _____

2. _____

3. _____

Today I Will Brighten _____'s Day By:

_____

_____

* * *

Today Was Great Because:

1. _____

2. _____

3. _____

Date: ___ / ___ / _____

"It's not the years in your life that count.
It's the life in your years."

– *Abraham Lincoln*

My Life Is Great Because:

1. _____

2. _____

3. _____

I Will Move Closer to My Goals Today By:

1. _____

2. _____

3. _____

Today I Will Brighten _____**'s Day By:**

_____

_____

* * *

Today Was Great Because:

1. _____

2. _____

3. _____

Date: ___ / ___ / _____

"Change your thoughts and you change your world."
— *Norman Vincent Peale*

My Life Is Great Because:

1. _____

2. _____

3. _____

I Will Move Closer to My Goals Today By:

1. _____

2. _____

3. _____

Today I Will Brighten _____**'s Day By:**

_____

_____

* * *

Today Was Great Because:

1. _____

2. _____

3. _____

Date: ___ / ___ / _____

"Either write something worth reading
or do something worth writing."
— *Benjamin Franklin*

My Life Is Great Because:

1. _____
2. _____
3. _____

I Will Move Closer to My Goals Today By:

1. _____
2. _____
3. _____

Today I Will Brighten _____'s Day By:

_____

_____

* * *

Today Was Great Because:

1. _____
2. _____
3. _____

Date: ___ / ___ / _____

"The only way to do great work is to love what you do."
— Steve Jobs

My Life Is Great Because:

1. _____

2. _____

3. _____

I Will Move Closer to My Goals Today By:

1. _____

2. _____

3. _____

Today I Will Brighten _____**'s Day By:**

_____

_____

* * *

Today Was Great Because:

1. _____

2. _____

3. _____

Date: ___ / ___ / _____

"We are what we repeatedly do. Excellence,
therefore, is not an act but a habit."

— Aristotle

My Life Is Great Because:

1. _____
2. _____
3. _____

I Will Move Closer to My Goals Today By:

1. _____
2. _____
3. _____

Today I Will Brighten _____**'s Day By:**

_____

_____

* * *

Today Was Great Because:

1. _____
2. _____
3. _____

Date: ___ / ___ / _____

"The best way out is always through."
— *Robert Frost*

My Life Is Great Because:

1. _____
2. _____
3. _____

I Will Move Closer to My Goals Today By:

1. _____
2. _____
3. _____

Today I Will Brighten _____'s Day By:

_____

_____

* * *

Today Was Great Because:

1. _____
2. _____
3. _____

Date: ___ / ___ / _____

"I know for sure that what we dwell
on is who we become."

— *Oprah Winfrey*

My Life Is Great Because:

1. _____

2. _____

3. _____

I Will Move Closer to My Goals Today By:

1. _____

2. _____

3. _____

Today I Will Brighten _____'s Day By:

_____

_____

* * *

Today Was Great Because:

1. _____

2. _____

3. _____

Date: ___ / ___ / _____

"You must be the change you want to see in the world."
— *Mahatma Gandhi*

My Life Is Great Because:

1. _____

2. _____

3. _____

I Will Move Closer to My Goals Today By:

1. _____

2. _____

3. _____

Today I Will Brighten _____'s Day By:

_____

_____

* * *

Today Was Great Because:

1. _____

2. _____

3. _____

Date: ___ / ___ / _____

"What you get by achieving your goals is not as important
as what you become by achieving your goals."

— *Goethe*

My Life Is Great Because:

1. _____
2. _____
3. _____

I Will Move Closer to My Goals Today By:

1. _____
2. _____
3. _____

Today I Will Brighten _____'s Day By:

_____

_____

* * *

Today Was Great Because:

1. _____
2. _____
3. _____

Date: ___ / ___ / _____

"You can get everything in life you want if you will just help enough other people get what they want."

– Zig Ziglar

My Life Is Great Because:

1. _____

2. _____

3. _____

I Will Move Closer to My Goals Today By:

1. _____

2. _____

3. _____

Today I Will Brighten _____**'s Day By:**

_____

_____

* * *

Today Was Great Because:

1. _____

2. _____

3. _____

Date: ___ / ___ / _____

"Desire is the starting point of all achievement, not a hope,
not a wish, but a keen pulsating desire which
transcends everything."

– Napoleon Hill

My Life Is Great Because:

1. _____

2. _____

3. _____

I Will Move Closer to My Goals Today By:

1. _____

2. _____

3. _____

Today I Will Brighten _____**'s Day By:**

_____

_____

* * *

Today Was Great Because:

1. _____

2. _____

3. _____

Date: ___ / ___ / _____

"Failure is the condiment that gives success its flavor."
– Truman Capote

My Life Is Great Because:

1. _____

2. _____

3. _____

I Will Move Closer to My Goals Today By:

1. _____

2. _____

3. _____

Today I Will Brighten _____'s Day By:

_____

_____

* * *

Today Was Great Because:

1. _____

2. _____

3. _____

Date: ___ / ___ / _____

"Vision without action is daydream.
Action without vision is nightmare."
— *Japanese Proverb*

My Life Is Great Because:

1. _____
2. _____
3. _____

I Will Move Closer to My Goals Today By:

1. _____
2. _____
3. _____

Today I Will Brighten _____'s Day By:

_____

_____

* * *

Today Was Great Because:

1. _____
2. _____
3. _____

Date: ___ / ___ / _____

"In any situation, the best thing you can do is the right thing; the next best thing you can do is the wrong thing; the worst thing you can do is nothing."
— *Theodore Roosevelt*

My Life Is Great Because:

1. _____

2. _____

3. _____

I Will Move Closer to My Goals Today By:

1. _____

2. _____

3. _____

Today I Will Brighten _____**'s Day By:**

_____

_____

* * *

Today Was Great Because:

1. _____

2. _____

3. _____

Date: ___ / ___ / _____

"Success consists of doing the common
things of life uncommonly well."

— Unknown

My Life Is Great Because:

1. _____

2. _____

3. _____

I Will Move Closer to My Goals Today By:

1. _____

2. _____

3. _____

Today I Will Brighten _____**'s Day By:**

_____

_____

* * *

Today Was Great Because:

1. _____

2. _____

3. _____

Date: ___ / ___ / _____

"Keep on going and the chances are you will stumble on something, perhaps when you are least expecting it. I have never heard of anyone stumbling on something sitting down."

— Charles F. Kettering

My Life Is Great Because:

1. _____

2. _____

3. _____

I Will Move Closer to My Goals Today By:

1. _____

2. _____

3. _____

Today I Will Brighten _____'s Day By:

_____

_____

* * *

Today Was Great Because:

1. _____

2. _____

3. _____

Date: ___ / ___ / _____

"Losers visualize the penalties of failure.
Winners visualize the rewards of success."

– Unknown

My Life Is Great Because:

1. _____

2. _____

3. _____

I Will Move Closer to My Goals Today By:

1. _____

2. _____

3. _____

Today I Will Brighten _____**'s Day By:**

_____

_____

* * *

Today Was Great Because:

1. _____

2. _____

3. _____

Date: ___ / ___ / _____

"Some succeed because they are destined.
Some succeed because they are determined."

— *Unknown*

My Life Is Great Because:

1. _____

2. _____

3. _____

I Will Move Closer to My Goals Today By:

1. _____

2. _____

3. _____

Today I Will Brighten _____'s Day By:

_____

_____

* * *

Today Was Great Because:

1. _____

2. _____

3. _____

Date: ___ / ___ / _____

"Experience is what you get when you
don't get what you want."

– *Dan Stanford*

My Life Is Great Because:

1. _____

2. _____

3. _____

I Will Move Closer to My Goals Today By:

1. _____

2. _____

3. _____

Today I Will Brighten _____'s Day By:

_____

_____

* * *

Today Was Great Because:

1. _____

2. _____

3. _____

Date: ___ / ___ / _____

"A happy person is not a person in a certain set of
circumstances, but rather a person with a
certain set of attitudes."

– Hugh Downs

My Life Is Great Because:

1. _____

2. _____

3. _____

I Will Move Closer to My Goals Today By:

1. _____

2. _____

3. _____

Today I Will Brighten _____'s Day By:

_____

_____

* * *

Today Was Great Because:

1. _____

2. _____

3. _____

Date: ___ / ___ / _____

"If you're going to be able to look back on something and laugh about it, you might as well laugh about it now."

— Marie Osmond

My Life Is Great Because:

1. _____

2. _____

3. _____

I Will Move Closer to My Goals Today By:

1. _____

2. _____

3. _____

Today I Will Brighten _____**'s Day By:**

_____

_____

* * *

Today Was Great Because:

1. _____

2. _____

3. _____

Date: ___ / ___ / _____

"Remember that happiness is a way
of travel, not a destination."

– Roy Goodman

My Life Is Great Because:

1. _____

2. _____

3. _____

I Will Move Closer to My Goals Today By:

1. _____

2. _____

3. _____

Today I Will Brighten _____**'s Day By:**

_____

_____

* * *

Today Was Great Because:

1. _____

2. _____

3. _____

Date: ___ / ___ / _____

"If you want to test your memory, try to recall what you
were worrying about one year ago today."

– *E. Joseph Cossman*

My Life Is Great Because:

1. _____
2. _____
3. _____

I Will Move Closer to My Goals Today By:

1. _____
2. _____
3. _____

Today I Will Brighten _____'s Day By:

_____

_____

***

Today Was Great Because:

1. _____
2. _____
3. _____

Date: ___ / ___ / _____

"What lies behind us and what lies before us are tiny
matters compared to what lies within us."

– Ralph Waldo Emerson

My Life Is Great Because:

1. _____

2. _____

3. _____

I Will Move Closer to My Goals Today By:

1. _____

2. _____

3. _____

Today I Will Brighten _____**'s Day By:**

_____

_____

* * *

Today Was Great Because:

1. _____

2. _____

3. _____

Date: ___ / ___ / _____

"The best way to cheer yourself up is to
try to cheer somebody else up."

– Mark Twain

My Life Is Great Because:

1. _____

2. _____

3. _____

I Will Move Closer to My Goals Today By:

1. _____

2. _____

3. _____

Today I Will Brighten _____'s Day By:

_____

_____

* * *

Today Was Great Because:

1. _____

2. _____

3. _____

Date: ___ / ___ / _____

"Take the first step in faith. You don't have to see the whole staircase, just take the first step."

– *Martin Luther King Jr.*

My Life Is Great Because:

1. _____

2. _____

3. _____

I Will Move Closer to My Goals Today By:

1. _____

2. _____

3. _____

Today I Will Brighten _____**'s Day By:**

_____

_____

* * *

Today Was Great Because:

1. _____

2. _____

3. _____

Date: ___ / ___ / _____

"Act or accept."

– *Anonymous*

My Life Is Great Because:

1. _____

2. _____

3. _____

I Will Move Closer to My Goals Today By:

1. _____

2. _____

3. _____

Today I Will Brighten _____'s Day By:

_____

_____

* * *

Today Was Great Because:

1. _____

2. _____

3. _____

Date: ___ / ___ / _____

"Many great ideas go unexecuted, and many great
executioners are without ideas.
One without the other is worthless."

– Tim Blixseth

My Life Is Great Because:

1. _____

2. _____

3. _____

I Will Move Closer to My Goals Today By:

1. _____

2. _____

3. _____

Today I Will Brighten _____'s Day By:

_____

_____

* * *

Today Was Great Because:

1. _____

2. _____

3. _____

Date: ___ / ___ / _____

"The world is more malleable than you think and it's
waiting for you to hammer it into shape."

— Bono

My Life Is Great Because:

1. _____

2. _____

3. _____

I Will Move Closer to My Goals Today By:

1. _____

2. _____

3. _____

Today I Will Brighten _____**'s Day By:**

_____

_____

* * *

Today Was Great Because:

1. _____

2. _____

3. _____

Date: ___ / ___ / _____

"Sometimes you just got to give yourself what
you wish someone else would give you."
– Dr. Phil

My Life Is Great Because:

1. _____

2. _____

3. _____

I Will Move Closer to My Goals Today By:

1. _____

2. _____

3. _____

Today I Will Brighten _____**'s Day By:**

_____

_____

* * *

Today Was Great Because:

1. _____

2. _____

3. _____

Date: ___ / ___ / _____

"Motivation is a fire from within. If someone else
tries to light that fire under you, chances are it
will burn very briefly."

– *Stephen R. Covey*

My Life Is Great Because:

1. _____

2. _____

3. _____

I Will Move Closer to My Goals Today By:

1. _____

2. _____

3. _____

Today I Will Brighten _____**'s Day By:**

_____

_____

* * *

Today Was Great Because:

1. _____

2. _____

3. _____

Date: ___ / ___ / _____

"People become really quite remarkable when they start thinking that they can do things. When they believe in themselves they have the first secret of success."

– Norman Vincent Peale

My Life Is Great Because:

1. _____
2. _____
3. _____

I Will Move Closer to My Goals Today By:

1. _____
2. _____
3. _____

Today I Will Brighten _____'s Day By:

_____

_____

* * *

Today Was Great Because:

1. _____
2. _____
3. _____

Date: ___ / ___ / _____

"Whenever you find whole world against you
just turn around and lead the world."

— *Anonymous*

My Life Is Great Because:

1. _____
2. _____
3. _____

I Will Move Closer to My Goals Today By:

1. _____
2. _____
3. _____

Today I Will Brighten _____**'s Day By:**

_____

_____

* * *

Today Was Great Because:

1. _____
2. _____
3. _____

Date: ___ / ___ / _____

"Being defeated is only a temporary condition;
giving up is what makes it permanent."

– Marilyn vos Savant

My Life Is Great Because:

1. _____

2. _____

3. _____

I Will Move Closer to My Goals Today By:

1. _____

2. _____

3. _____

Today I Will Brighten _____**'s Day By:**

_____

_____

* * *

Today Was Great Because:

1. _____

2. _____

3. _____

Date: ___ / ___ / _____

"I can't understand why people are frightened
by new ideas. I'm frightened by old ones."

– John Cage

My Life Is Great Because:

1. _____

2. _____

3. _____

I Will Move Closer to My Goals Today By:

1. _____

2. _____

3. _____

Today I Will Brighten _____'s Day By:

_____

_____

* * *

Today Was Great Because:

1. _____

2. _____

3. _____

Date: ___ / ___ / _____

"The difference between ordinary and
extraordinary is that little extra."

– Unknown

My Life Is Great Because:

1. _____

2. _____

3. _____

I Will Move Closer to My Goals Today By:

1. _____

2. _____

3. _____

Today I Will Brighten _____'s Day By:

_____

_____

* * *

Today Was Great Because:

1. _____

2. _____

3. _____

Date: ___ / ___ / _____

"The best way to predict the future is to create it."

– Unknown

My Life Is Great Because:

1. _____

2. _____

3. _____

I Will Move Closer to My Goals Today By:

1. _____

2. _____

3. _____

Today I Will Brighten _____**'s Day By:**

_____

_____

***

Today Was Great Because:

1. _____

2. _____

3. _____

Date: ___ / ___ / _____

"Anyone can do something when they *want* to do it. Really
successful people do things when they don't want to do it."

— Dr. Phil

My Life Is Great Because:

1. _____

2. _____

3. _____

I Will Move Closer to My Goals Today By:

1. _____

2. _____

3. _____

Today I Will Brighten _____'s Day By:

_____

_____

* * *

Today Was Great Because:

1. _____

2. _____

3. _____

Date: ___ / ___ / _____

"There are two primary choices in life: to accept conditions as they exist, or accept the responsibility for changing them."

– Dr. Denis Waitley

My Life Is Great Because:

1. _____
2. _____
3. _____

I Will Move Closer to My Goals Today By:

1. _____
2. _____
3. _____

Today I Will Brighten _____'s Day By:

_____

_____

* * *

Today Was Great Because:

1. _____
2. _____
3. _____

Date: ___ / ___ / _____

"Success is the ability to go from failure to failure
without losing your enthusiasm."

— Sir Winston Churchill

My Life Is Great Because:

1. _____

2. _____

3. _____

I Will Move Closer to My Goals Today By:

1. _____

2. _____

3. _____

Today I Will Brighten _____'s Day By:

_____

_____

* * *

Today Was Great Because:

1. _____

2. _____

3. _____

Date: ___ / ___ / _____

"Success seems to be connected with action. Successful
people keep moving. They make mistakes but don't quit."
– *Conrad Hilton*

My Life Is Great Because:

1. _____
2. _____
3. _____

I Will Move Closer to My Goals Today By:

1. _____
2. _____
3. _____

Today I Will Brighten _____**'s Day By:**

_____

_____

* * *

Today Was Great Because:

1. _____
2. _____
3. _____

Date: ___ / ___ / _____

"Attitudes are contagious.
Make yours worth catching."

– Unknown

My Life Is Great Because:

1. _____

2. _____

3. _____

I Will Move Closer to My Goals Today By:

1. _____

2. _____

3. _____

Today I Will Brighten _____'s Day By:

_____

_____

* * *

Today Was Great Because:

1. _____

2. _____

3. _____

Date: ___ / ___ / _____

"Do not let what you cannot do interfere
with what you can do."

– John Wooden

My Life Is Great Because:

1. _____

2. _____

3. _____

I Will Move Closer to My Goals Today By:

1. _____

2. _____

3. _____

Today I Will Brighten _____'s Day By:

_____

_____

* * *

Today Was Great Because:

1. _____

2. _____

3. _____

Date: ___ / ___ / _____

"There are only two rules for being successful. One, figure out exactly what you want to do, and two, do it."

— *Mario Cuomo*

My Life Is Great Because:

1. _____

2. _____

3. _____

I Will Move Closer to My Goals Today By:

1. _____

2. _____

3. _____

Today I Will Brighten _____**'s Day By:**

_____

_____

* * *

Today Was Great Because:

1. _____

2. _____

3. _____

Date: ___ / ___ / _____

"Sooner or later, those who win are
those who think they can."

— Richard Bach

My Life Is Great Because:

1. _____

2. _____

3. _____

I Will Move Closer to My Goals Today By:

1. _____

2. _____

3. _____

Today I Will Brighten _____'s Day By:

_____

_____

* * *

Today Was Great Because:

1. _____

2. _____

3. _____

Date: ___ / ___ / _____

"Success is a state of mind. If you want success, start thinking of yourself as a success."

– Dr. Joyce Brothers

My Life Is Great Because:

1. _____

2. _____

3. _____

I Will Move Closer to My Goals Today By:

1. _____

2. _____

3. _____

Today I Will Brighten _____'s Day By:

_____

_____

* * *

Today Was Great Because:

1. _____

2. _____

3. _____

Date: ___ / ___ / _____

My Life Is Great Because:

1. _____
2. _____
3. _____

I Will Move Closer to My Goals Today By:

1. _____
2. _____
3. _____

Today I Will Brighten _____**'s Day By:**

_____

_____

* * *

Today Was Great Because:

1. _____
2. _____
3. _____

Date: ___ / ___ / _____

"Winners lose much more often than losers.
So if you keep losing but you're still trying, keep it up!
You're right on track."
— *Matthew Keith Groves*

My Life Is Great Because:

1. _____

2. _____

3. _____

I Will Move Closer to My Goals Today By:

1. _____

2. _____

3. _____

Today I Will Brighten _____'s Day By:

_____

_____

* * *

Today Was Great Because:

1. _____

2. _____

3. _____

Date: ___ / ___ / _____

"An obstacle is often a stepping stone."
– *William Prescott*

My Life Is Great Because:

1. _____
2. _____
3. _____

I Will Move Closer to My Goals Today By:

1. _____
2. _____
3. _____

Today I Will Brighten _____'s Day By:

_____

_____

* * *

Today Was Great Because:

1. _____
2. _____
3. _____

Date: ___ / ___ / _____

"Life is 'trying things to see if they work.'"
– *Ray Bradbury*

My Life Is Great Because:

1. _____

2. _____

3. _____

I Will Move Closer to My Goals Today By:

1. _____

2. _____

3. _____

Today I Will Brighten _____'s Day By:

_____

_____

* * *

Today Was Great Because:

1. _____

2. _____

3. _____

Date: ___ / ___ / _____

"Strength does not come from physical capacity.
It comes from an indomitable will."

– *Mahatma Gandhi*

My Life Is Great Because:

1. _____

2. _____

3. _____

I Will Move Closer to My Goals Today By:

1. _____

2. _____

3. _____

Today I Will Brighten _____'s Day By:

_____

_____

***

Today Was Great Because:

1. _____

2. _____

3. _____

Date: ___ / ___ / _____

"What you do speaks so loudly that
I cannot hear what you say."
— Ralph Waldo Emerson

My Life Is Great Because:

1. _____
2. _____
3. _____

I Will Move Closer to My Goals Today By:

1. _____
2. _____
3. _____

Today I Will Brighten _____**'s Day By:**

_____

_____

* * *

Today Was Great Because:

1. _____
2. _____
3. _____

Date: ___ / ___ / _____

"Success is not to be measured by the position someone has reached in life, but the obstacles he has overcome while trying to succeed."

– *Booker T. Washington*

My Life Is Great Because:

1. _____

2. _____

3. _____

I Will Move Closer to My Goals Today By:

1. _____

2. _____

3. _____

Today I Will Brighten _____**'s Day By:**

_____

_____

* * *

Today Was Great Because:

1. _____

2. _____

3. _____

Date: ___ / ___ / _____

"To avoid criticism, do nothing, say nothing, be nothing."
— *Elbert Hubbard*

My Life Is Great Because:

1. _____
2. _____
3. _____

I Will Move Closer to My Goals Today By:

1. _____
2. _____
3. _____

Today I Will Brighten _____'s Day By:

_____

_____

* * *

Today Was Great Because:

1. _____
2. _____
3. _____

Date: ___ / ___ / _____

"If you want to make your dreams come true,
the first thing you have to do is wake up."

– *J.M. Power*

My Life Is Great Because:

1. _____

2. _____

3. _____

I Will Move Closer to My Goals Today By:

1. _____

2. _____

3. _____

Today I Will Brighten _____**'s Day By:**

_____

_____

* * *

Today Was Great Because:

1. _____

2. _____

3. _____

Date: ___ / ___ / _____

"I've learned that people will forget what you said, people
will forget what you did, but people will
never forget how you made them feel."

– Maya Angelou

My Life Is Great Because:

1. _____
2. _____
3. _____

I Will Move Closer to My Goals Today By:

1. _____
2. _____
3. _____

Today I Will Brighten _____**'s Day By:**

_____

_____

* * *

Today Was Great Because:

1. _____
2. _____
3. _____

Date: ___ / ___ / _____

"I attribute my success to this: I never
gave or took any excuse."
— *Florence Nightingale*

My Life Is Great Because:

1. _____

2. _____

3. _____

I Will Move Closer to My Goals Today By:

1. _____

2. _____

3. _____

Today I Will Brighten _____'s Day By:

_____

_____

* * *

Today Was Great Because:

1. _____

2. _____

3. _____

Date: ___ / ___ / _____

"I've learned that no matter what happens, or how bad
it seems today, life does go on, and it will be
better tomorrow."

– Maya Angelou

My Life Is Great Because:

1. _____

2. _____

3. _____

I Will Move Closer to My Goals Today By:

1. _____

2. _____

3. _____

Today I Will Brighten _____**'s Day By:**

_____

_____

* * *

Today Was Great Because:

1. _____

2. _____

3. _____

Date: ___ / ___ / _____

"The art of being wise is the art of
knowing what to overlook."

– *William James*

My Life Is Great Because:

1. _____
2. _____
3. _____

I Will Move Closer to My Goals Today By:

1. _____
2. _____
3. _____

Today I Will Brighten _____'s Day By:

_____

_____

***

Today Was Great Because:

1. _____
2. _____
3. _____

Date: ___ / ___ / _____

"You gain strength, courage and confidence by every experience in which you stop to look fear in the face."

– Eleanor Roosevelt

My Life Is Great Because:

1. _____

2. _____

3. _____

I Will Move Closer to My Goals Today By:

1. _____

2. _____

3. _____

Today I Will Brighten _____'s Day By:

_____

_____

* * *

Today Was Great Because:

1. _____

2. _____

3. _____

Date: ___ / ___ / _____

"Do first things first, and second things not at all."

– Peter Drucker

My Life Is Great Because:

1. _____

2. _____

3. _____

I Will Move Closer to My Goals Today By:

1. _____

2. _____

3. _____

Today I Will Brighten _____'s Day By:

_____

_____

* * *

Today Was Great Because:

1. _____

2. _____

3. _____

Date: ___ / ___ / _____

"I am an optimist. It does not seem too
much use being anything else."

– *Winston Churchill*

My Life Is Great Because:

1. _____

2. _____

3. _____

I Will Move Closer to My Goals Today By:

1. _____

2. _____

3. _____

Today I Will Brighten _____'s Day By:

_____

_____

* * *

Today Was Great Because:

1. _____

2. _____

3. _____

Date: ___ / ___ / _____

"If you're going through hell, keep going."
— *Winston Churchill*

My Life Is Great Because:

1. _____

2. _____

3. _____

I Will Move Closer to My Goals Today By:

1. _____

2. _____

3. _____

Today I Will Brighten _____**'s Day By:**

_____

_____

* * *

Today Was Great Because:

1. _____

2. _____

3. _____

Date: ___ / ___ / _____

"There is no education like adversity."
– Disraeli

My Life Is Great Because:

1. _____

2. _____

3. _____

I Will Move Closer to My Goals Today By:

1. _____

2. _____

3. _____

Today I Will Brighten _____**'s Day By:**

_____

_____

* * *

Today Was Great Because:

1. _____

2. _____

3. _____

Date: ___ / ___ / _____

"Try to be a rainbow in someone's cloud."

– *Maya Angelou*

My Life Is Great Because:

1. _____

2. _____

3. _____

I Will Move Closer to My Goals Today By:

1. _____

2. _____

3. _____

Today I Will Brighten _____'s Day By:

_____

_____

* * *

Today Was Great Because:

1. _____

2. _____

3. _____

Date: ___ / ___ / _____

"I dwell in possibility."
— *Emily Dickinson*

My Life Is Great Because:

1. _____

2. _____

3. _____

I Will Move Closer to My Goals Today By:

1. _____

2. _____

3. _____

Today I Will Brighten _____**'s Day By:**

_____

_____

* * *

Today Was Great Because:

1. _____

2. _____

3. _____

Date: ___ / ___ / _____

"I believe purpose is something for which one is
responsible; it's not just divinely assigned."
— Michael J. Fox

My Life Is Great Because:

1. _____

2. _____

3. _____

I Will Move Closer to My Goals Today By:

1. _____

2. _____

3. _____

Today I Will Brighten _____**'s Day By:**

_____

_____

* * *

Today Was Great Because:

1. _____

2. _____

3. _____

Date: ___ / ___ / _____

"Lean forward into your life. Begin
each day as if it were on purpose."

– *Mary Anne Radmacher*

My Life Is Great Because:

1. _____
2. _____
3. _____

I Will Move Closer to My Goals Today By:

1. _____
2. _____
3. _____

Today I Will Brighten _____'s Day By:

_____

_____

***

Today Was Great Because:

1. _____
2. _____
3. _____

Date: ___ / ___ / _____

"You never regret being kind."
— Nicole Shepherd

My Life Is Great Because:

1. _____

2. _____

3. _____

I Will Move Closer to My Goals Today By:

1. _____

2. _____

3. _____

Today I Will Brighten _____'s Day By:

_____

_____

* * *

Today Was Great Because:

1. _____

2. _____

3. _____

Date: ___ / ___ / _____

"People who use time wisely spend it on activities that advance their overall purpose in life."

— *John C. Maxwell*

My Life Is Great Because:

1. _____
2. _____
3. _____

I Will Move Closer to My Goals Today By:

1. _____
2. _____
3. _____

Today I Will Brighten _____**'s Day By:**

_____

_____

* * *

Today Was Great Because:

1. _____
2. _____
3. _____

Date: ___ / ___ / _____

"No man or woman is an island. To exist just for yourself is meaningless. You can achieve the most satisfaction when you feel related to some greater purpose in life, something greater than yourself."

— Denis Waitley

My Life Is Great Because:

1. _____

2. _____

3. _____

I Will Move Closer to My Goals Today By:

1. _____

2. _____

3. _____

Today I Will Brighten _____'s Day By:

_____

_____

* * *

Today Was Great Because:

1. _____

2. _____

3. _____

Date: ___ / ___ / _____

"The art of living lies less in eliminating
our troubles than growing with them."
– *Bernard M. Baruch*

My Life Is Great Because:

1. _____

2. _____

3. _____

I Will Move Closer to My Goals Today By:

1. _____

2. _____

3. _____

Today I Will Brighten _____**'s Day By:**

_____

_____

* * *

Today Was Great Because:

1. _____

2. _____

3. _____

Date: ___ / ___ / _____

"When you stay on purpose and refuse to be discouraged by fear, you align with the infinite self, in which all possibilities exist."

– Wayne Dyer

My Life Is Great Because:

1. _____

2. _____

3. _____

I Will Move Closer to My Goals Today By:

1. _____

2. _____

3. _____

Today I Will Brighten _____**'s Day By:**

_____

_____

* * *

Today Was Great Because:

1. _____

2. _____

3. _____

Date: ___ / ___ / _____

"To retain the loyalty of those who are present,
be loyal to those who are absent."
— *Stephen R. Covey*

My Life Is Great Because:

1. _____

2. _____

3. _____

I Will Move Closer to My Goals Today By:

1. _____

2. _____

3. _____

Today I Will Brighten _____**'s Day By:**

_____

_____

* * *

Today Was Great Because:

1. _____

2. _____

3. _____

Date: ___ / ___ / _____

"Every saint has a past; every sinner has a future."
– *Oscar Wilde*

My Life Is Great Because:

1. _____
2. _____
3. _____

I Will Move Closer to My Goals Today By:

1. _____
2. _____
3. _____

Today I Will Brighten _____**'s Day By:**

_____

_____

* * *

Today Was Great Because:

1. _____
2. _____
3. _____

Date: ___ / ___ / _____

"The only place where success comes
before work is in the dictionary."

— *Vidal Sasson*

My Life Is Great Because:

1. _____

2. _____

3. _____

I Will Move Closer to My Goals Today By:

1. _____

2. _____

3. _____

Today I Will Brighten _____'s Day By:

_____

_____

* * *

Today Was Great Because:

1. _____

2. _____

3. _____

Date: ___ / ___ / _____

"Ability is what you're capable of doing.
Motivation determines what you do.
Attitude determines how well you do it."

– Lou Holtz

My Life Is Great Because:

1. _____

2. _____

3. _____

I Will Move Closer to My Goals Today By:

1. _____

2. _____

3. _____

Today I Will Brighten _____'s Day By:

_____

_____

* * *

Today Was Great Because:

1. _____

2. _____

3. _____

Date: ___ / ___ / _____

"A grateful heart is a beginning of greatness. It is an
expression of humility. It is a foundation for the
development of such virtues as prayer, faith, courage,
contentment, happiness, love, and well-being."
– James E. Faust

My Life Is Great Because:

1. _____
2. _____
3. _____

I Will Move Closer to My Goals Today By:

1. _____
2. _____
3. _____

Today I Will Brighten _____**'s Day By:**

_____

_____

* * *

Today Was Great Because:

1. _____
2. _____
3. _____

Date: ___ / ___ / _____

"In life, adversity only visits the strong. It stays forever
with the weak. We have to decide whether
we're going to be strong or weak."

– Dale Brown

My Life Is Great Because:

1. _____

2. _____

3. _____

I Will Move Closer to My Goals Today By:

1. _____

2. _____

3. _____

Today I Will Brighten _____**'s Day By:**

_____

_____

***

Today Was Great Because:

1. _____

2. _____

3. _____

Date: ___ / ___ / _____

"If people are doubting how far you'll go,
go so far that you can't hear them anymore."
– Michele Ruiz

My Life Is Great Because:

1. _____
2. _____
3. _____

I Will Move Closer to My Goals Today By:

1. _____
2. _____
3. _____

Today I Will Brighten _____'s Day By:

_____

_____

* * *

Today Was Great Because:

1. _____
2. _____
3. _____

Date: ___ / ___ / _____

"You have to be willing to get your heart broken to be a champion, and you have to do it over and over again."

— *Doc Rivers*

My Life Is Great Because:

1. _____
2. _____
3. _____

I Will Move Closer to My Goals Today By:

1. _____
2. _____
3. _____

Today I Will Brighten _____**'s Day By:**

_____

_____

* * *

Today Was Great Because:

1. _____
2. _____
3. _____

Date: ___ / ___ / _____

"When you're good at something, you'll tell everyone.
When you're great at something, they'll tell you."
— *Walter Payton*

My Life Is Great Because:

1. _____

2. _____

3. _____

I Will Move Closer to My Goals Today By:

1. _____

2. _____

3. _____

Today I Will Brighten _____**'s Day By:**

_____

_____

* * *

Today Was Great Because:

1. _____

2. _____

3. _____

Date: ___ / ___ / _____

"If it's important you'll find a way.
If it's not, you'll find an excuse."

– *Ryan Blair*

My Life Is Great Because:

1. _____

2. _____

3. _____

I Will Move Closer to My Goals Today By:

1. _____

2. _____

3. _____

Today I Will Brighten _____'s Day By:

_____

_____

* * *

Today Was Great Because:

1. _____

2. _____

3. _____

Date: ___ / ___ / _____

"It is amazing what you can accomplish if
you do not care who gets the credit."
— *Harry Truman*

My Life Is Great Because:

1. _____

2. _____

3. _____

I Will Move Closer to My Goals Today By:

1. _____

2. _____

3. _____

Today I Will Brighten _____**'s Day By:**

_____

_____

* * *

Today Was Great Because:

1. _____

2. _____

3. _____

Date: ___ / ___ / _____

"It had long since come to my attention that people of accomplishment rarely sat back and let things happen to them. They went out and happened to things."

– Leonardo da Vinci

My Life Is Great Because:

1. _____

2. _____

3. _____

I Will Move Closer to My Goals Today By:

1. _____

2. _____

3. _____

Today I Will Brighten _____'s Day By:

_____

_____

***

Today Was Great Because:

1. _____

2. _____

3. _____

Date: ___ / ___ / _____

"The 3C's in Life: Choice, Chance, Change.
You must make the choice, to take the chance,
if you want anything in life to change."

– Unknown

My Life Is Great Because:

1. _____

2. _____

3. _____

I Will Move Closer to My Goals Today By:

1. _____

2. _____

3. _____

Today I Will Brighten _____'s Day By:

_____

_____

* * *

Today Was Great Because:

1. _____

2. _____

3. _____

Date: ___ / ___ / _____

> "Dream as if you'll live forever,
> live as if you'll die today."
>
> — *James Dean*

My Life Is Great Because:

1. _____

2. _____

3. _____

I Will Move Closer to My Goals Today By:

1. _____

2. _____

3. _____

Today I Will Brighten _____'s Day By:

_____

_____

* * *

Today Was Great Because:

1. _____

2. _____

3. _____

Date: ___ / ___ / _____

"Be happy with what you have.
Be excited about what you want."

— *Alan Cohen*

My Life Is Great Because:

1. _____

2. _____

3. _____

I Will Move Closer to My Goals Today By:

1. _____

2. _____

3. _____

Today I Will Brighten _____**'s Day By:**

_____

_____

* * *

Today Was Great Because:

1. _____

2. _____

3. _____

Date: ___ / ___ / _____

"Much of the stress that people feel doesn't come from having too much to do. It comes from not finishing what they've started."

— David Allen

My Life Is Great Because:

1. _____

2. _____

3. _____

I Will Move Closer to My Goals Today By:

1. _____

2. _____

3. _____

Today I Will Brighten _____**'s Day By:**

_____

_____

* * *

Today Was Great Because:

1. _____

2. _____

3. _____

Date: ___ / ___ / _____

"I can accept failure, everyone fails at something.
But I can't accept not trying."
– Michael Jordan

My Life Is Great Because:

1. _____

2. _____

3. _____

I Will Move Closer to My Goals Today By:

1. _____

2. _____

3. _____

Today I Will Brighten _____**'s Day By:**

_____

_____

* * *

Today Was Great Because:

1. _____

2. _____

3. _____

Date: ___ / ___ / _____

"Everything is a gift of the universe--even joy, anger,
jealously, frustration, or separateness. Everything is
perfect either for our growth or our enjoyment."

— Ken Keyes

My Life Is Great Because:

1. _____

2. _____

3. _____

I Will Move Closer to My Goals Today By:

1. _____

2. _____

3. _____

Today I Will Brighten _____**'s Day By:**

_____

_____

* * *

Today Was Great Because:

1. _____

2. _____

3. _____

Date: ___ / ___ / _____

"Great minds have purposes, others have wishes."
– Washington Irving

My Life Is Great Because:

1. _____
2. _____
3. _____

I Will Move Closer to My Goals Today By:

1. _____
2. _____
3. _____

Today I Will Brighten _____'s Day By:

_____

_____

* * *

Today Was Great Because:

1. _____
2. _____
3. _____

Date: ___ / ___ / _____

"Thousands of candles can be lit from a single candle,
and the life of the candle will not be shortened.
Happiness never decreases by being shared."

— *Buddha*

My Life Is Great Because:

1. _____

2. _____

3. _____

I Will Move Closer to My Goals Today By:

1. _____

2. _____

3. _____

Today I Will Brighten _____**'s Day By:**

_____

_____

* * *

Today Was Great Because:

1. _____

2. _____

3. _____

Date: ___ / ___ / _____

"The right way is not always the popular and easy way.
Standing for right when it is unpopular is a true test
of moral character."

– Margaret Chase Smith

My Life Is Great Because:

1. _____
2. _____
3. _____

I Will Move Closer to My Goals Today By:

1. _____
2. _____
3. _____

Today I Will Brighten _____'s Day By:

_____

_____

* * *

Today Was Great Because:

1. _____
2. _____
3. _____

Date: ___ / ___ / _____

"Everything that irritates us about others can lead
us to an understanding of ourselves."

– Carl Jung

My Life Is Great Because:

1. _____

2. _____

3. _____

I Will Move Closer to My Goals Today By:

1. _____

2. _____

3. _____

Today I Will Brighten _____**'s Day By:**

_____

_____

* * *

Today Was Great Because:

1. _____

2. _____

3. _____

Date: ___ / ___ / _____

"We make a living by what we get,
we make a life by what we give."

— Winston Churchill

My Life Is Great Because:

1. _____
2. _____
3. _____

I Will Move Closer to My Goals Today By:

1. _____
2. _____
3. _____

Today I Will Brighten _____'s Day By:

_____

_____

* * *

Today Was Great Because:

1. _____
2. _____
3. _____

Date: ___ / ___ / _____

"Happiness is not having what you want.
It is appreciating what you have."

– Unknown

My Life Is Great Because:

1. _____

2. _____

3. _____

I Will Move Closer to My Goals Today By:

1. _____

2. _____

3. _____

Today I Will Brighten _____**'s Day By:**

_____

_____

* * *

Today Was Great Because:

1. _____

2. _____

3. _____

Date: ___ / ___ / _____

"If you want others to be happy, practice compassion.
If you want to be happy, practice compassion."

– Dalai Lama

My Life Is Great Because:

1. _____

2. _____

3. _____

I Will Move Closer to My Goals Today By:

1. _____

2. _____

3. _____

Today I Will Brighten _____'s Day By:

_____

_____

* * *

Today Was Great Because:

1. _____

2. _____

3. _____

CONGRATS!

You've just completed a solid six months of daily journaling. How do you feel? Have you noticed an impact? Have you brightened others' days, developed a deeper sense of gratitude, and made measurable progress toward your goals?

If so, **please consider leaving a review on Amazon.com.** Doing so helps others discover this journal and invite greater success and satisfaction into their own lives.

I would also love to hear from you! If you have questions, thoughts, or stories of success, shoot me an email at michael@3minutemorning.com. This daily practice has made a significant difference in my life, and few things bring me greater joy than hearing from others who have experienced the same.

Remember: you are the master of your life. You get to decide how you spend your time, how you see the world, and how you interact with those around you. You've no-doubt accomplished great things in the past six months. Don't stop now! Grab another journal and keep the momentum you've built. You live an amazing life. Soak it in. Appreciate it. Then continue the work of making it even better.

Made in the USA
Las Vegas, NV
26 February 2021